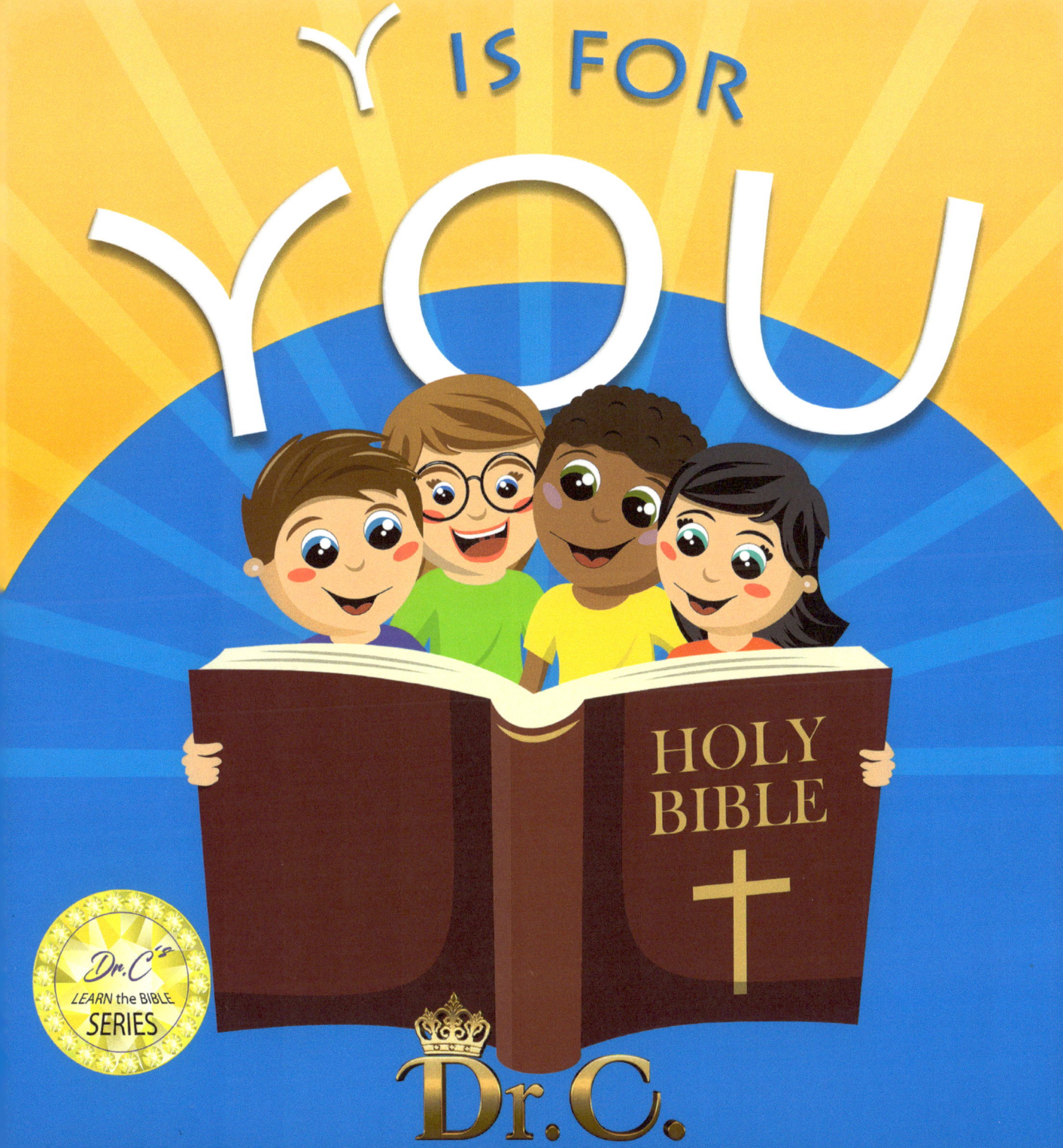

www.clfpublishing.org
909.315.3161

Copyright © 2022 by Cassundra White-Elliott.

All rights reserved. No portion of this book may be reproduced, stored in a retrieval system, or transmitted by any form or any means electronically, photocopied, recorded, or any other except for brief quotations in printed reviews, without the prior permission of the publisher.

Cover design by Senir Design. Contact info: info@senirdesign.com

ISBN #978-1-945102-85-1

Printed in the United States of America.

Dedicated

to all the students at

Excellence Academy

"I praise you, for I am fearfully and wonderfully made. Wonderful are your works; my soul knows it very well."
Psalm 139:14 (ESV)

Be happy because everything God makes is wonderful. You are God's unique design. There is no one who is exactly like you. That makes you very special. You are beautiful, strong, smart, loving, kind, and funny.

"What is mankind that you are mindful of them, human beings that you care for them? You have made them a little lower than the angels and crowned them with glory and honor."
Psalm 8:4-5 (NIV)

Angels are with God in Heaven. They are very special to Him. When God created mankind, He made them just a little lower than the angels, which means they are very important and special to God as well. God loves and cares for all of His creation.

"But you are not like that, for you are a chosen people. You are royal priests, a holy nation, God's very own possession. As a result, you can show others the goodness of God, for he called you out of the darkness into his wonderful light."
I Peter 2:9 (NIV)

The Bible says God is the King of Kings and the Lord of Lords. You are a child of the King! So, you are royalty. As a child of the King, tell others how good God has been to you. Ask your friends if they want to be part of God's family too.

*"For God has not given us a spirit of fear,
but of power, love, and self-control."*

II Timothy 1:7 (BSB)

There are many things that can be scary, but God wants us to trust Him and be strong at all times. Sometimes, we don't feel as though we can handle everything that comes our way. But, we must trust and depend on God. He is with us at all times.

"Love the Lord *your God with all your heart and with all your soul and with all your strength."*
Deuteronomy 6:5 (NIV)

Loving God means loving His Word. Do you have a Bible? Did you know there are Bibles written just for kids? Try to read your Bible every day or at least a few days a week. Ask your mother or father to read the Bible with you.

"Honor your father and your mother, so that you may live long in the land the LORD your God is giving you."

Exodus 20:12 (NIV)

God is happy when you honor your parents by listening to what they tell you and by doing what they tell you to do. Be respectful to your parents. Do not speak rudely to them or be disobedient. When you treat your parents with respect, God will allow you to live a long time.

"Don't let anyone look down on you because you are young, but set an example for the believers in speech, in conduct, in love, in faith and in purity."
I Timothy 4:12 (NIV)

Just because you may be younger than other people does not mean you don't have something important to say. However, when you speak, be respectful of other people, and they will listen to you when you talk. Speak with respect, love, and kindness.

Add your picture into the frame.

When you look at it, you will see a child of God,

whom God loves very much.

www.ingramcontent.com/pod-product-compliance
Lightning Source LLC
Chambersburg PA
CBHW041933160426
42813CB00103B/2901